# TAGAKI

多書き

TAGAKI（多書き）とは、一言で言えば、「英語で自分を表現することを学ぶための、ボルダリング競技みたいなもの」です。その足場はメンタル面と英語面の2種類で、この足場を使って登って行き頂上を目指しましょう。このTAGAKIでは、考える→書く→伝えるを30トピック繰り返すことで、自分の意見を持ち、英語を書けるようになります。そうすると世界に飛び出して行けそうな自分を感じることができるでしょう。

# TAGAKI 30 Contents もくじ

| | | |
|---|---|---|
| このワークブックの進め方 | | 4 |

| Topics | | Categories | |
|---|---|---|---|
| 1 | **Big Dinner**（たっぷりの夕食） | Life | 6 |
| 2 | **Car Racing**（カーレース） | Sport | 8 |
| 3 | **Childhood**（子ども時代） | Life | 10 |
| 4 | **Chorus**（コーラス） | Music | 12 |
| 5 | **Cooking**（料理） | Food | 14 |
| 6 | **Country**（田舎） | Places | 16 |
| 7 | **Fish**（魚） | Food | 18 |
| 8 | **Friendly**（フレンドリーな人） | Personality | 20 |
| 9 | **Good Dreams**（良い夢） | Personality | 22 |
| 10 | **Grasshoppers**（キリギリスタイプの人） | Personality | 24 |
| 11 | **Hairstyle**（髪型） | Fashion | 26 |
| 12 | **Hot Summers**（暑い夏） | Seasons | 28 |
| 13 | **Last Day of School**（学校最後の日） | School Life | 30 |
| 14 | **Lost and Found**（落としもの） | Life | 32 |
| 15 | **Melody**（メロディー） | Music | 34 |
| 16 | **Moon**（月） | Space | 36 |
| 17 | **Morning**（朝） | Technology | 38 |
| 18 | **New Year's Day**（お正月） | Seasons | 40 |
| 19 | **Night Sky**（夜空） | Nature | 42 |
| 20 | **Outdoors**（アウトドア派） | Life | 44 |
| 21 | **Parties**（パーティー） | Personality | 46 |

| 22 | **Quiet**（静かに） | Life | 48 |
| 23 | **Robot Engineers**（ロボットエンジニア） | Technology | 50 |
| 24 | **Speakers**（話し上手な人） | Personality | 52 |
| 25 | **Sprinting**（短距離走） | Sport | 54 |
| 26 | **Summer Vacation**（夏休み） | Life | 56 |
| 27 | **Sweets**（スイーツ） | Food | 58 |
| 28 | **Toyama Prefecture**（富山県） | Places | 60 |
| 29 | **Trains**（列車） | Personality | 62 |
| 30 | **Winning**（勝つこと） | Life | 64 |

**進度表** 終わったトピックの番号に印をつけていきましょう！

# TAGAKI 30 をはじめよう

TAGAKI 30から英作文の構成を学んでいきます。自分ではない人物になりきり、自分が何を表現したいかを客観的に考えることを学んでいきましょう。最後の1行で自分の意見も述べていきます。

## 進め方

**文の構成**

- **Catchy Sentences（つかみ）**：これからこのような話をすると、端的に相手にわからせ、ひきつけることを書きます。
- **Facts（事実）**：つかみを裏付ける説明や事実関係、理由などを書きます。
- **Punch Lines（おち）**：話のしめくくりになることを書きます。

**Step 1**（Thinking／Reading）
トピックについて考えましょう。Sample Sentences を読み、見本文の人はどんな人か考えます。次に自分だったらどうかなと考えながら Words and Phrases A B を見ます。

**Step 2**（Listening）
Sample Sentences と Words and Phrases と My Opinion の音声をQRコードできくことができます。音声をチェックしましょう。

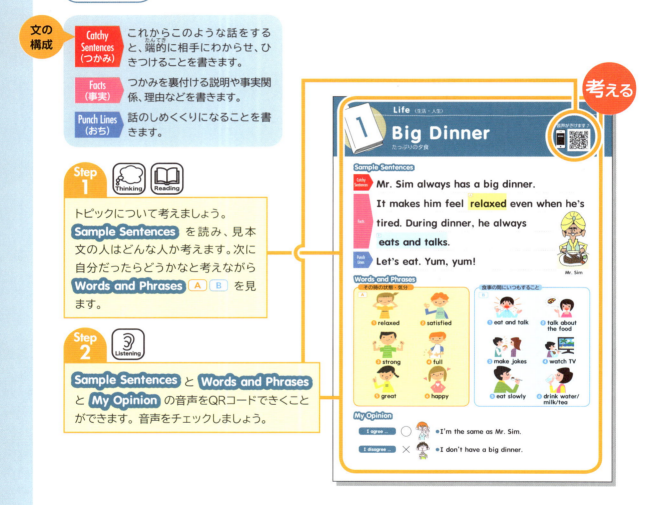

**1人でTAGAKIを学ぶ人へ**
単独の良さをいかし、自由に自分のペースでStep1〜5を進んでください。自分で自分の進歩を見届け、それぞれの目的や目標、例えば入試や検定試験、会議やプレゼンなどのために書く力を付けてください。

# TAGAKI 30目標

| メンタル | 相手に伝わる構成を身に付ける 最後に賛成か反対かを表明する |
|---|---|

文の構成(「つかみ」「事実」「おち」)をマスターしましょう。最後に、見本文の人に賛成意見か反対意見か、ヒントを参考に自分の意見を書きましょう。

| 英語 | 30語前後の英文で「なりきりライティング」 |
|---|---|

見本文の人になったつもりで「なりきりライティング」をしましょう。見本文の3人称を1人称に変更するところに気を付けながら、様々な30人になりきって自分のことのように書いてみましょう。

**Step 3**  Writing

**Sample Sentences** 例「Mr.Sim」を「I」の1人称の文章にかえて、 **Words and Phrases**   から自分に当てはまるものを選び、入れかえて全文を書き写しましょう。

○は1人称にかえたところです。トピック18、28、29は自分の家族にかえ、トピック30は自分のチームにかえましょう。

**Step 4**  Writing  Speaking

**Writing Time** ❶ で書いた文を見ないで、もう一度書きましょう。書いた文を覚えて声に出して言いましょう。

**Step 5**  Writing  Speaking

**Sample Sentences** の人と自分とで違うところはどこかを考え、 **My Opinion** を参考にI agree …(賛成)かI disagree …(反対)か、自分の意見を **Writing Time** ❸ に書きましょう。書いた文を覚えて声に出して言いましょう。

| ペアやグループでTAGAKIを学ぶ人へ | Step1〜5を進めた後、友達や家族、先生に向けて発表したり、他の人の発表を聞いて、英語または日本語でディスカッションしたりして、4技能の学習へ発展してください。書いたものは見ないで発表しましょう。 |
|---|---|

## Life 〈生活・人生〉

# Big Dinner
たっぷりの夕食

音声がきけます♪

## Sample Sentences

**Catchy Sentences:** Mr. Sim always has a big dinner.

**Facts:** It makes him feel **relaxed** (A) even when he's tired. During dinner, he always **eats and talks.** (B)

**Punch Lines:** Let's eat. Yum, yum!

Mr. Sim

## Words and Phrases

その時の状態・気分 (A)

1. relaxed
2. satisfied
3. strong
4. full
5. great
6. happy

食事の間にいつもすること (B)

1. eat and talk
2. talk about the food
3. make jokes
4. watch TV
5. eat slowly
6. drink water/milk/tea

## My Opinion

**I agree ...** ○ • I'm the same as Mr. Sim.

**I disagree ...** × • I don't have a big dinner.

TAGAKI 30

## Writing Time

**1** Mr. Sim のようにいつもたくさん夕食をとる人になったつもりで Ⓐ と Ⓑ を入れかえて全文を書こう。

Catchy Sentences

Facts

Punch Lines

**2** 上で書いた文を見ないで書いて、見ないで言おう。

Catchy Sentences

Facts

Punch Lines

**3** **My Opinion** を参考に自分の意見を書いて、見ないで言おう。

7

## 2 Sport 〈スポーツ〉
# Car Racing
カーレース

 音声がきけます♪

### Sample Sentences

**Catchy Sentences:** Azi loves car racing.

**Facts:** Someday, he wants to go to [A] the USA to see the famous car race. It's one of [B] the coolest car races in the world.

**Punch Lines:** The engine sounds shake Azi's heart!

Azi

### Words and Phrases

行きたい国

❶ the USA  ❷ Monaco  ❸ France  ❹ Peru  ❺ Germany  ❻ Argentina

カーレースの様子

❶ the coolest  ❷ the longest  ❸ the fastest  ❹ the loudest  ❺ the most expensive  ❻ the most dangerous

### My Opinion

I agree ...  ○  ● I love car racing, too.

I disagree ...  ×  ● I'm different from Azi.

8

TAGAKI 30

## Writing Time

**1** Azi のようにカーレースが好きな人になったつもりで Ⓐ と Ⓑ を入れかえて全文を書こう。

Catchy
Sentences

Facts

Punch
Lines

**2** 上で書いた文を見ないで書いて、見ないで言おう。

Catchy
Sentences

Facts

Punch
Lines

**3** **My Opinion** を参考に自分の意見を書いて、見ないで言おう。

9

# 3 Life 〈生活・人生〉
## Childhood
子ども時代

音声がきけます♪

## Sample Sentences

**Catchy Sentences**: Bella thinks children enjoy their lives more than adults do.

**Facts**: Children [A] study more and grow wiser. They have [B] more imagination, which makes their lives more enjoyable.

**Punch Lines**: Childhood is the best time of life!

Bella

## Words and Phrases

子どもがすること

① study more  ② read more
③ play more  ④ sleep more
⑤ eat more  ⑥ laugh more

子どもが持っているもの

① more imagination  ② more dreams
③ more time  ④ more freedom
⑤ more curiosity  ⑥ more fun

## My Opinion

 I agree ... ○ • I also think children enjoy their lives more than adults do.

 I disagree ... × • I don't think children study more.

# TAGAKI に関するお知らせ

## TAGAKI [10〜50] の音声がQRコードで聴けるようになりました！

### 今まで音声を聞くときは…
「mpi オトキコ」アプリをインストール

### 改訂後、音声を聞くときは…
「QR コード」でより簡単になりました！

「mpi オトキコ」から「QR コード」へは順次切り替えいたします。そのため、10〜50 のレベルによって切り替えのタイミングが異なることを何卒ご了承願います。

※QR コードは（株）デンソーウェーブの登録商標です。

 株式会社mpi松香フォニックス　www.mpi-j.co.jp

TAGAKI 30

## Writing Time

**1** Bella のように子どものほうが（大人より）人生を楽しんでいると思う人になったつもりで 🅰 と 🅱 を入れかえて全文を書こう。

Catchy
Sentences

Facts

Punch
Lines

**2** 上で書いた文を見ないで書いて、見ないで言おう。

Catchy
Sentences

Facts

Punch
Lines

**3** **My Opinion** を参考に自分の意見を書いて、見ないで言おう。

11

# 4 Music 〈音楽〉
## Chorus
コーラス

音声がきけます♪

## Sample Sentences

**Catchy Sentences**: Chadi thinks singing together is a lot of fun.

**Facts**: In the future, he wants to join a pop chorus group. He hopes his group will someday perform in New York.

**Punch Lines**: Let's sing la, la, la, la!

Chadi

## Words and Phrases

参加したいグループ

A
1. a pop chorus group
2. a gospel chorus group
3. a dancing and singing chorus group
4. the school chorus club
5. a community chorus group
6. a professional chorus group

発表したい場所

B
1. in New York
2. at Tokyo Dome
3. on TV
4. at a school festival
5. at a local festival
6. at a concert hall

## My Opinion

I agree ... ○ ・In the future, I also want to join a pop chorus group.

I disagree ... × ・I don't think singing together is a lot of fun.

## Writing Time

**1** Chadi のようにみんなで歌うことがとても楽しいと思う人になったつもりで [A]
と [B] を入れかえて全文を書こう。

Catchy
Sentences

Facts

Punch
Lines

**2** 上で書いた文を見ないで書いて、見ないで言おう。

Catchy
Sentences

Facts

Punch
Lines

**3** **My Opinion** を参考に自分の意見を書いて、見ないで言おう。

# 5 Food 〈食べもの〉
## Cooking
料理

## Sample Sentences

**Catchy Sentences:** Didi sometimes cooks on weekends.

**Facts:** When she cooks homemade pizza [A], everybody is glad. She wants to cook more often and surprise her friends [B].

**Punch Lines:** Some people eat to live, and others live to eat.

Didi

## Words and Phrases

時々作る料理 [A]
1. homemade pizza
2. spicy fried chicken
3. my special spaghetti
4. rice
5. miso soup
6. noodles

びっくりさせたい人 [B]
1. grandma/grandpa
2. mom/dad
3. brother/sister
4. cousins
5. friends
6. boyfriend/girlfriend

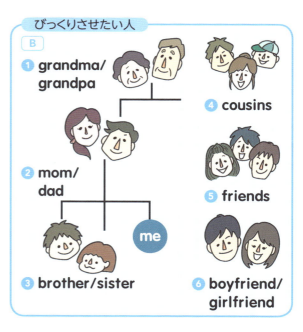

## My Opinion

- I agree ... ○ ● I sometimes cook on weekends, too.
- I disagree ... × ● I don't cook homemade pizza.

14

## Writing Time

**1** Didi のように週末に時々料理をする人になったつもりで [A]　と　[B]　を入れかえて全文を書こう。

**Catchy Sentences**

**Facts**

**Punch Lines**

**2** 上で書いた文を見ないで書いて、見ないで言おう。

**Catchy Sentences**

**Facts**

**Punch Lines**

**3** **My Opinion** を参考に自分の意見を書いて、見ないで言おう。

**Places** 〈場所〉

# Country
田舎(いなか)

音声がきけます♪

## Sample Sentences

**Catchy Sentences**: In the future, Enam wants to live in the country.

**Facts**:
She thinks the country is **healthier**. [A]
In the country, she'll enjoy **growing vegetables**. [B]

**Punch Lines**: Ah, breathe that fresh country air!

Enam

## Words and Phrases

田舎について思うこと [A]

1. healthier
2. quieter
3. slower
4. cheaper
5. friendlier
6. more peaceful

田舎で楽しむこと [B]

1. growing vegetables
2. chatting with neighbors
3. eating fresh eggs
4. going mountain climbing
5. going to the local festivals
6. going on a mushroom hunt

## My Opinion

**I agree ...** ○ • In the future, I want to live in the country, too.

**I disagree ...** × • In the country, I won't enjoy growing vegetables.

16

## Writing Time

**1** Enam のように将来、田舎（いなか）に住みたい人になったつもりで [A] と [B] を入れかえて全文を書こう。

| | |
|---|---|
| Catchy Sentences | |
| Facts | |
| Punch Lines | |

**2** 上で書いた文を見ないで書いて、見ないで言おう。

| | |
|---|---|
| Catchy Sentences | |
| Facts | |
| Punch Lines | |

**3** **My Opinion** を参考に自分の意見を書いて、見ないで言おう。

17

# 1 Food 〈食べもの〉

## Fish
魚

### Sample Sentences

**Catchy Sentences:** When someone asks Fui, "Would you like fish or meat?" she always answers, "Fish, please."

**Facts:** She likes  sashimi . Eating fish will make her  smart .

**Punch Lines:** Thank you, fish!

Fui

### Words and Phrases

好きな魚料理

① sashimi (raw fish)
② sushi
③ grilled salmon
④ fish and chips
⑤ fried fish
⑥ dried fish

魚の栄養・効果

① smart
② strong
③ good-looking
④ slim
⑤ active
⑥ relaxed

### My Opinion

**I agree ...** ○ ● I like sashimi, too.

**I disagree ...** × ● When someone asks me, "Would you like fish or meat?" I never answer, "Fish, please."

# TAGAKI 30

## Writing Time

**1** Fui のように魚料理か、肉料理かを聞かれたら、いつも魚料理と答える人になった
つもりで Ⓐ と Ⓑ を入れかえて全文を書こう。

**Catchy Sentences**

**Facts**

**Punch Lines**

**2** 上で書いた文を見ないで書いて、見ないで言おう。

**Catchy Sentences**

**Facts**

**Punch Lines**

**3** **My Opinion** を参考に自分の意見を書いて、見ないで言おう。

19

**Personality** 〈パーソナリティー〉

# Friendly
フレンドリーな人

音声がきけます♪

## Sample Sentences

**Catchy Sentences** Fal is a friendly person.

**Facts** He's always [A] calm . He often [B] says hello to people.

**Punch Lines** Let's make the world a better place.

Fal

## Words and Phrases

性格

[A]
1. calm
2. gentle
3. kind
4. peaceful
5. cheerful
6. quiet

人によくすること

[B]
1. say hello to
2. smile at
3. talk to
4. call
5. send emails to
6. ask questions of

## My Opinion

I agree ... ○ ・I often say hello to people, too.

I disagree ... × ・I'm shy, but I make people happy in my own way.

20

TAGAKI 30

## Writing Time

**1** Fal のようにフレンドリーな人になったつもりで [A] と [B] を入れかえて全文を書こう。

Catchy
Sentences

Facts

Punch
Lines

**2** 上で書いた文を見ないで書いて、見ないで言おう。

Catchy
Sentences

Facts

Punch
Lines

**3** **My Opinion** を参考に自分の意見を書いて、見ないで言おう。

21

## 9. Personality 〈パーソナリティー〉
# Good Dreams
良い夢

### Sample Sentences

**Catchy Sentences:** Imm always has good dreams.

**Facts:** In one of her good dreams, she **got a perfect score in a test**. In another good dream, she **flew like a bird**.

**Punch Lines:** She's so lucky!

Imm

### Words and Phrases
良い夢

1. got a perfect score in a test
2. won a soccer match
3. did a good presentation
4. passed the university entrance exam
5. wrote a good essay
6. finished the project on time
7. flew like a bird
8. met a person I've really wanted to meet
9. talked with Napoleon Bonaparte
10. sang with my favorite singer
11. won the lottery
12. became a famous artist

### My Opinion

**I agree ...** ○ • I flew like a bird in my dream, too.

**I disagree ...** × • In my dream, I didn't get a perfect score.

**TAGAKI 30**

## Writing Time

**1** Imm のようにいつも良い夢を見る人になったつもりで ▨Ａ と ▨Ｂ を入れかえて全文を書こう。

**Catchy Sentences**

**Facts**

**Punch Lines**

**2** 上で書いた文を見ないで書いて、見ないで言おう。

**Catchy Sentences**

**Facts**

**Punch Lines**

**3** **My Opinion** を参考に自分の意見を書いて、見ないで言おう。

23

## Personality 〈パーソナリティー〉

# 10 Grasshoppers
キリギリスタイプの人

音声がきけます♪

### Sample Sentences

**Catchy Sentences** ▶ Mim is a grasshopper-type person.

**Facts** ▶ The grasshopper says, "Play now and work later." She <u>listens to music</u> [A] first and then <u>worries</u> [B].

**Punch Lines** ▶ All work and no play makes Jack a dull boy!

Mim

### Words and Phrases

始めにすること

A
① listen to music
② check my emails
③ take a nap
④ play games
L
⑤ eat snacks
⑥ play with my pet

その後すること

B
① worry
② do the chores
③ practice calligraphy/ soccer/the piano
④ do my homework
⑤ clean my room
⑥ have regrets

### My Opinion

I agree ...  ○   ● I truly enjoy my life, too.

I disagree ...  ×   ● I'm not a grasshopper-type person.

24

## Writing Time

**1** Mim のようにキリギリスタイプの人になったつもりで **A** と **B** を入れかえて全文を書こう。

**Catchy Sentences**

**Facts**

**Punch Lines**

**2** 上で書いた文を見ないで書いて、見ないで言おう。

**Catchy Sentences**

**Facts**

**Punch Lines**

**3** **My Opinion** を参考に自分の意見を書いて、見ないで言おう。

## 11 Fashion 〈ファッション〉
# Hairstyle
髪型(かみがた)

音声がきけます♪

### Sample Sentences

**Catchy Sentences:** Jox is really fond of his hairstyle.

**Facts:** He has  long hair . He dyed his hair  dark brown.

**Punch Lines:** He thinks he's too cool for school!

Jox

### Words and Phrases

髪型(かみがた)

❶ long hair　❷ straight hair　❸ curly hair　❹ short hair　❺ braids　❻ a pony tail

染めている髪(かみ)の色

❶ dark brown　❷ blond　❸ silver　❹ light brown　❺ rainbow colors　❻ partly purple

### My Opinion

I agree ... 〇　● I'm really fond of my hairstyle, too.

I disagree ... ✕　● Hairstyle isn't a big issue in life.

26

TAGAKI 30

## Writing Time

**1** Jox のように自分の髪型(かみがた)がとても好きな人になったつもりで Ⓐ と Ⓑ を入れかえて全文を書こう。

**Catchy Sentences**

**Facts**

**Punch Lines**

**2** 上で書いた文を見ないで書いて、見ないで言おう。

**Catchy Sentences**

**Facts**

**Punch Lines**

**3** **My Opinion** を参考に自分の意見を書いて、見ないで言おう。

27

# 12 Seasons 〈季節〉
## Hot Summers
暑い夏

音声がきけます♪

### Sample Sentences

**Catchy Sentences:** Our teacher Mr. Han likes a hot summer.

**Facts:** He enjoys **swimming in the sea**. He's careful, too. He makes sure to **drink a lot of water**.

**Punch Lines:** Ah, it's nice and hot!

Mr. Han

### Words and Phrases

夏に楽しむこと
A
1. swimming in the sea
2. going surfing
3. going camping
4. attending training camps
5. having barbeques
6. playing beach volleyball

必ずすること
B
1. drink a lot of water
2. wear a big hat
3. put on sun screen
4. wear sunglasses
5. rest in the shade
6. take a cold shower

### My Opinion

**I agree ...** ○ ● I'm looking forward to a hot summer!

**I disagree ...** × ● I don't enjoy swimming in the sea.

28

## Writing Time

**1** Mr. Han のように暑い夏が好きな人になったつもりで [A] と [B] を入れかえて全文を書こう。

Catchy Sentences

Facts

Punch Lines

**2** 上で書いた文を見ないで書いて、見ないで言おう。

Catchy Sentences

Facts

Punch Lines

**3** **My Opinion** を参考に自分の意見を書いて、見ないで言おう。

# 13 School Life 〈学校生活〉

## Last Day of School
学校最後の日

音声がきけます♪

### Sample Sentences

**Catchy Sentences:** Nam still remembers her last day of elementary school.

**Facts:** She clearly remembers giving [A] **an album** to the teachers. She was very [B] **sad**.

**Punch Lines:** She misses her school so much!

Nam

### Words and Phrases

先生にあげたもの

[A]

1. an album
2. hugs
3. some presents
4. messages
5. letters
6. some flowers

その時の気持ち

[B]

1. sad
2. overexcited
3. happy
4. nervous
5. calm
6. lonely

### My Opinion

 ○  I also miss my school so much.

 ×  Elementary school is a distant memory.

## Writing Time

**1** Nam のように学校最後の日をまだ覚えている人になったつもりで ⒶＡ と ⒷＢ を入れかえて全文を書こう。

| | |
|---|---|
| **Catchy Sentences** | |
| **Facts** | |
| **Punch Lines** | |

**2** 上で書いた文を見ないで書いて、見ないで言おう。

| | |
|---|---|
| **Catchy Sentences** | |
| **Facts** | |
| **Punch Lines** | |

**3** **My Opinion** を参考に自分の意見を書いて、見ないで言おう。

# 14 Life 〈生活・人生〉

## Lost and Found
落としもの

### Sample Sentences

**Catchy Sentences:** This is a true story of lost and found.

**Facts:** One day, Mr. Natt lost his **bicycle key**. He couldn't find it anywhere. He was very shocked.

**Punch Lines:** Later, he found it **in his shoe!**

Mr. Natt

### Words and Phrases

なくしたもの

1. bicycle key
2. car key
3. house key
4. mobile phone
5. commuter pass
6. wallet

見つかった場所

1. in my shoe
2. under the table
3. in the toilet
4. in the washing machine
5. in the fridge
6. in my pocket

### My Opinion

I agree ... ○ ● One day, I lost my bicycle key, too.

I disagree ... × ● This story is crazy/foolish/unbelievable.

TAGAKI 30

## Writing Time

**1** Mr. Natt のように落としものをして、見つけた人になったつもりで A と
B を入れかえて全文を書こう。

Catchy
Sentences

Facts

Punch
Lines

**2** 上で書いた文を見ないで書いて、見ないで言おう。

Catchy
Sentences

Facts

Punch
Lines

**3** **My Opinion** を参考に自分の意見を書いて、見ないで言おう。

33

# 15 Music 〈音楽〉

## Melody
メロディー

音声がきけます♪

## Sample Sentences

**Catchy Sentences**: Kiki loves making beautiful melodies.

**Facts**: She plays [A] the violin with a lot of feeling.

Her family always [B] turns off the TV when she practices.

**Punch Lines**: Her family is the best!

Kiki

## Words and Phrases

演奏する楽器

[A]
1. the violin
2. the piano
3. the keyboard
4. the recorder
5. the cello
6. the flute

家族がいつもすること

[B]
1. turn off the TV
2. come to listen
3. say, "Please be quiet."
4. close the door
5. open the windows
6. give me a big hand

## My Opinion

**I agree ...** ○ ● I play the violin with a lot of feeling, too.

**I disagree ...** × ● I just play the music the way it's written.

## Writing Time

**1** Kiki のように美しいメロディーを奏でるのが好きな人になったつもりで Ⓐ と
Ⓑ を入れかえて全文を書こう。

Catchy Sentences

Facts

Punch Lines

**2** 上で書いた文を見ないで書いて、見ないで言おう。

Catchy Sentences

Facts

Punch Lines

**3** **My Opinion** を参考に自分の意見を書いて、見ないで言おう。

## Space 〈宇宙〉

# Moon
月

音声がきけます♪

### Sample Sentences

**Catchy Sentences**: If Luz gets a chance, he'll go to the moon.

**Facts**: He wants to walk on the moon. But the trip to the moon will cost so much money that he'll have to save money first.

**Punch Lines**: It's going to be tough!

Luz

### Words and Phrases

したいこと

① walk on the moon
② see the Earth from there
③ make a giant leap
④ drive a space car
⑤ feel excited at the time of blast off
⑥ eat space food

始めにしなくてはならないこと

① save money
② win the lottery
③ find a job
④ study English and Russian
⑤ find a sponsor
⑥ go through hard training

### My Opinion

I agree ...  ○  • I'll have to save money first, too.

I disagree ...  ×  • Even if I get a chance, I won't go to the moon.

# Writing Time

**1** Luz のように機会があれば、月に行きたいと思っている人になったつもりで Ⓐ と Ⓑ を入れかえて全文を書こう。

**Catchy Sentences**

**Facts**

**Punch Lines**

**2** 上で書いた文を見ないで書いて、見ないで言おう。

**Catchy Sentences**

**Facts**

**Punch Lines**

**3** **My Opinion** を参考に自分の意見を書いて、見ないで言おう。

# 17 Technology 〈テクノロジー〉

## Morning
朝

音声がきけます♪

## Sample Sentences

**Catchy Sentences**: Mia is always too busy in the morning.

**Facts**: She believes that she has to **take a shower** [A] before she leaves home. She wants a robot that will **cook her breakfast**. [B]

**Punch Lines**: That would be awesome!

Mia

## Words and Phrases

朝、家を出る前にしなければならないこと [A]

ロボットにしてほしいこと [B]

1. take a shower
2. hang out the laundry
3. brush my teeth
4. finish my homework
5. do my hair
6. check the weather

1. cook my breakfast
2. iron my shirt
3. polish my shoes
4. prepare my lunch
5. tidy my desk
6. play music for me

## My Opinion

**I agree ...** ○  ● I'm always too busy in the morning, too.

**I disagree ...** ✕  ● I think that morning should be a relaxing time.

**TAGAKI 30**

## Writing Time

**1** Mia のようにいつも朝は忙しい人になったつもりで [A] と [B] を入れかえて全文を書こう。

**Catchy Sentences**

**Facts**

**Punch Lines**

**2** 上で書いた文を見ないで書いて、見ないで言おう。

**Catchy Sentences**

**Facts**

**Punch Lines**

**3** **My Opinion** を参考に自分の意見を書いて、見ないで言おう。

39

## 18 Seasons 〈季節〉
# New Year's Day
お正月

### Sample Sentences

**Catchy Sentences**: In Gon's family, they all like New Year's Day.

**Facts**: They like eating osechi, the special New Year's food. They look forward to going to a shrine.

**Punch Lines**: Happy New Year!

Gon's family

### Words and Phrases

好きな正月料理
A
1. osechi, the special New Year's food
2. rice cakes
3. ozoni, the special New Year's soup
4. sea bream
5. black beans
6. radish and carrot salad

楽しみにしていること
B
1. going to a shrine
2. having a big family party
3. getting some New Year's money
4. going to get a lucky bag
5. watching TV all day
6. doing nothing

### My Opinion

I agree ... ○ ●In my family, we all like New Year's Day, too.

I disagree ... × ●We get too lazy to go to a shrine.

TAGAKI 30

## Writing Time

**1** Gon's family のように家族全員がお正月を好きな人になったつもりで Ⓐ　　　 と
Ⓑ　　　 を入れかえて全文を書こう。

**Catchy Sentences**

**Facts**

**Punch Lines**

**2** 上で書いた文を見ないで書いて、見ないで言おう。

**Catchy Sentences**

**Facts**

**Punch Lines**

**3** **My Opinion** を参考に自分の意見を書いて、見ないで言おう。

41

## Nature 〈自然〉

# Night Sky
夜空

音声がきけます♪

### Sample Sentences

**Catchy Sentences:** Raj likes looking up at the night sky.

**Facts:** He thinks the night sky is the most beautiful with <u>a full moon</u> [A]. He thinks the night sky is the best <u>in spring</u> [B].

**Punch Lines:** Yawn! Good night!

Raj

### Words and Phrases

夜空を一番美しくするもの
A
1. a full moon
2. the twinkling stars
3. a shooting star
4. the Milky Way
5. a total eclipse
6. a crescent moon

最高の季節・場所
B
1. in spring
2. in summer
3. in autumn (fall)
4. in winter
5. on the beach
6. on top of a mountain

### My Opinion

**I agree ...** ○ • I also think the night sky is the most beautiful with a full moon.

**I disagree ...** × • The night sky is only dark, after all.

**TAGAKI 30**

## Writing Time

**1** Raj のように夜空を見上げるのが好きな人になったつもりで A と B を入れかえて全文を書こう。

Catchy Sentences

Facts

Punch Lines

**2** 上で書いた文を見ないで書いて、見ないで言おう。

Catchy Sentences

Facts

Punch Lines

**3** My Opinion を参考に自分の意見を書いて、見ないで言おう。

43

## 20 Life 〈生活・人生〉

# Outdoors
アウトドア派

音声がきけます♪

### Sample Sentences

**Catchy Sentences**: My grandpa likes going outdoors a lot.

**Facts**: He likes [A] the beach. He feels happy when he [B] goes fishing.

**Punch Lines**: It's such a great feeling to be in nature.

my grandpa

### Words and Phrases

好きな場所 [A]

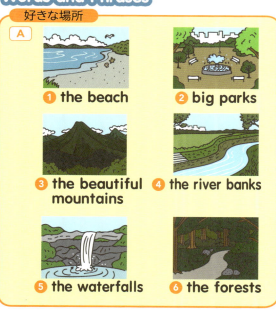

❶ the beach  ❷ big parks
❸ the beautiful mountains  ❹ the river banks
❺ the waterfalls  ❻ the forests

幸せを感じる時 [B]

❶ go fishing  ❷ go swimming
❸ ride my bike  ❹ go jogging
❺ have a barbeque party  ❻ go rock climbing

### My Opinion

 I agree ...   ○  ● I feel happy when I go fishing, too.

 I disagree ...  ×  ● I think that the outdoors are full of danger.

44

TAGAKI 30

## Writing Time

**1** my grandpa のようにアウトドア派の人になったつもりで [A] と [B] を入れかえて全文を書こう。

**Catchy Sentences**

**Facts**

**Punch Lines**

**2** 上で書いた文を見ないで書いて、見ないで言おう。

**Catchy Sentences**

**Facts**

**Punch Lines**

**3** **My Opinion** を参考に自分の意見を書いて、見ないで言おう。

45

**Personality** 〈パーソナリティー〉

# 21 Parties
パーティー

音声がきけます♪

## Sample Sentences

**Catchy Sentences:** Mof is a party person. She loves parties.

**Facts:** Of course, she goes to a lot of **birthday parties**[A]. What she likes most about parties is the **surprising costumes**[B].

**Punch Lines:** Let's party!

Mof

## Words and Phrases

よく行くパーティー

[A]
1. birthday parties
2. Halloween parties
3. Christmas parties
4. welcome parties
5. farewell parties
6. anniversary parties

一番好きなもの

[B]
1. surprising costumes
2. good food and drink
3. decorations
4. fun people
5. nice places
6. good jokes

## My Opinion

 I agree ... ○ • I love parties, too.

I disagree ... × • Parties are tiring for me.

# Writing Time

**1** Mof のようにパーティーが好きな人になったつもりで [A]　　 と [B]　　 を入れかえて全文を書こう。

**Catchy Sentences**

**Facts**

**Punch Lines**

**2** 上で書いた文を見ないで書いて、見ないで言おう。

**Catchy Sentences**

**Facts**

**Punch Lines**

**3** **My Opinion** を参考に自分の意見を書いて、見ないで言おう。

# 22 Life 〈生活・人生〉

## Quiet
静かに

音声がきけます♪

## Sample Sentences

**Catchy Sentences:** When my cousin Sid feels stressed, he likes to stay quiet.

**Facts:** He stays in his room and <mark>reads comics</mark>. [A]

He sometimes plays with his pet, too. [B]

**Punch Lines:** This is how he makes himself feel better.

Sid

## Words and Phrases

部屋の中ですること [A]

① read comics
② listen to music
③ fiddle with my mobile phone
④ play games
⑤ go to bed and sleep
⑥ think quietly

時々すること [B]

① play with my pet
② eat my favorite snacks
③ do nothing
④ watch TV
⑤ practice handstands
⑥ draw pictures

## My Opinion

 I agree ...　○　● I stay in my room and read comics, too.

 I disagree ...　×　● When I feel stressed, I don't like to stay quiet.

# Writing Time

**1** Sid のようにストレスを感じた時、静かにしているのが好きな人になったつもりで A
と B を入れかえて全文を書こう。

**Catchy Sentences**

**Facts**

**Punch Lines**

**2** 上で書いた文を見ないで書いて、見ないで言おう。

**Catchy Sentences**

**Facts**

**Punch Lines**

**3** **My Opinion** を参考に自分の意見を書いて、見ないで言おう。

49

## 23 Technology 〈テクノロジー〉

# Robot Engineers
ロボットエンジニア

 音声がきけます♪

### Sample Sentences

**Catchy Sentences** ▸ Ulla wants to be a robot engineer.

**Facts** ▸ She's interested in making cute robot pets such as baby pandas. She also wants to help people walk.

**Punch Lines** ▸ Welcome to the future!

Ulla

### Words and Phrases

ペットロボットの種類

① baby pandas   ② kittens
③ puppies       ④ baby bears
⑤ dolphins      ⑥ little birds

ロボットが助けられること

① walk          ② carry heavy things
③ get up        ④ take a seat
⑤ eat           ⑥ take a bath

### My Opinion

   ● I'm also interested in making cute robot pets.

  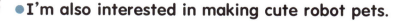 ● Being a robot engineer sounds too difficult for me.

TAGAKI 30

## Writing Time

**1** Ulla のようにロボットエンジニアになりたい人になったつもりで [A] と [B] を入れかえて全文を書こう。

**Catchy Sentences**

**Facts**

**Punch Lines**

**2** 上で書いた文を見ないで書いて、見ないで言おう。

**Catchy Sentences**

**Facts**

**Punch Lines**

**3** **My Opinion** を参考に自分の意見を書いて、見ないで言おう。

51

# 24 Personality 〈パーソナリティー〉

## Speakers
話し上手な人

音声がきけます♪

## Sample Sentences

**Catchy Sentences** > Ves is a good speaker.

**Facts** > She talks a lot and she's **expressive**. [A]

She often says, "**Fantastic!**" [B]

**Punch Lines** > Good speakers make everybody smile.

Ves

## Words and Phrases

**性格** [A]

① expressive　② open-minded
③ positive　④ sociable
⑤ happy　⑥ energetic

**よく言うこと** [B]

① Fantastic!　② Exactly!
③ That's a good idea.　④ I agree with you.
⑤ That's a miracle!　⑥ You can do it!

## My Opinion

 I agree ...　○　　● I like to make everybody smile.

 I disagree ...　✕　　● I don't talk a lot and I'm not expressive.

52

# TAGAKI 30

## Writing Time

**1** Ves のように話し上手な人になったつもりで ⒜ と ⒝ を入れかえて
全文を書こう。

| Catchy Sentences | |
| --- | --- |
| Facts | |
| Punch Lines | |

**2** 上で書いた文を見ないで書いて、見ないで言おう。

| Catchy Sentences | |
| --- | --- |
| Facts | |
| Punch Lines | |

**3** **My Opinion** を参考に自分の意見を書いて、見ないで言おう。

53

Sport 〈スポーツ〉

# 25 Sprinting
短距離走

音声がきけます♪

## Sample Sentences

**Catchy Sentences**: Po thinks sprinting is a lot of fun.

**Facts**: He practices sprinting with the track and field club. Someday, he wants to go to Jamaica to see the best training.

**Punch Lines**: Okay! Whoosh!

Po

## Words and Phrases

練習するところ

A
1. with the track and field club
2. in the playground
3. on the steps at home
4. in the gym
5. on the steps at a shrine
6. on a hill

行きたい国

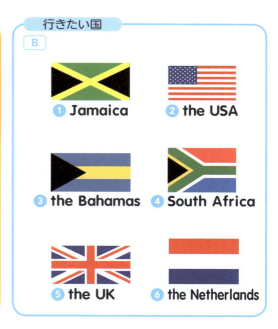

B
1. Jamaica
2. the USA
3. the Bahamas
4. South Africa
5. the UK
6. the Netherlands

## My Opinion

I agree ... ○ • I also want to go to Jamaica to see the best training.

I disagree ... × • I don't have the muscles for sprinting.

TAGAKI 30

## Writing Time

**1** Po のように短距離走がとても楽しいと思う人になったつもりで A と B を入れかえて全文を書こう。

Catchy
Sentences

Facts

Punch
Lines

**2** 上で書いた文を見ないで書いて、見ないで言おう。

Catchy
Sentences

Facts

Punch
Lines

**3** **My Opinion** を参考に自分の意見を書いて、見ないで言おう。

55

Life 〈生活・人生〉

# Summer Vacation
夏休み

 音声がきけます♪

## Sample Sentences

**Catchy Sentences**: Zui thinks summer vacation is a challenging time.

**Facts**: He wants to [A] **start something new**. At the same time, he's trying not to [B] **go to bed late**.

**Punch Lines**: Give it a try!

 Zui

## Words and Phrases

挑戦したいこと
[A]
1. start something new
2. travel alone
3. go to bed early
4. attend some special events
5. cook once a week
6. read more books

しないようにすること
[B]
1. go to bed late
2. get too lazy
3. play too many games
4. keep saying, "It's hot!"
5. ignore my homework
6. eat and drink too much

## My Opinion

 I agree ... ○ ● I'm also going to try not to go to bed late.

 I disagree ... × ● I don't want to start something new, because it's just too hot.

## Writing Time

**1** Zui のように夏休みが挑戦の時だと思う人になったつもりで [A] と [B] を入れかえて全文を書こう。

**Catchy Sentences**

**Facts**

**Punch Lines**

**2** 上で書いた文を見ないで書いて、見ないで言おう。

**Catchy Sentences**

**Facts**

**Punch Lines**

**3** **My Opinion** を参考に自分の意見を書いて、見ないで言おう。

# 27 Food 〈食べもの〉
## Sweets
スイーツ

音声がきけます♪

## Sample Sentences

**Catchy Sentences**: Ms. Wad loves sweet things.

**Facts**: For example, she likes **chocolate** [A] very much. But she knows sweet things are bad for her, so she tries to have **fruit** [B] instead.

**Punch Lines**: She's doing her best!

Ms. Wad

## Words and Phrases

好きなもの [A]

1. chocolate
2. cake
3. parfait
4. candy
5. pancakes
6. pie

代わりに食べるもの [B]

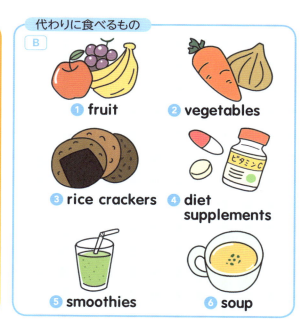

1. fruit
2. vegetables
3. rice crackers
4. diet supplements
5. smoothies
6. soup

## My Opinion

I agree ... ○ ● I like chocolate very much, too.

I disagree ... × ● I don't think sweet things are bad for me.

58

## Writing Time

**1** Ms. Wad のようにあまいものが好きな人になったつもりで [A] と [B] を入れかえて全文を書こう。

Catchy Sentences

Facts

Punch Lines

**2** 上で書いた文を見ないで書いて、見ないで言おう。

Catchy Sentences

Facts

Punch Lines

**3** **My Opinion** を参考に自分の意見を書いて、見ないで言おう。

# 28

## Places 〈場所〉

## Toyama Prefecture
富山県

音声がきけます♪

## Sample Sentences

**Catchy Sentences:** Wym's family is planning a trip to Toyama Prefecture.

**Facts:** They'll visit the famous places, for example, the Kurobe Dam. They'll also enjoy riding the trolley trains.

**Punch Lines:** It's an awesome place!

Wym's family

## Words and Phrases

有名な場所

A
1. the Kurobe Dam
2. Mount Tsurugi
3. Toyama Bay
4. the Snow Wall (Yuki-no-Otani)
5. the Tateyama Kurobe Alpine Route
6. Gokayama

体験したいこと

B
1. riding the trolley trains
2. riding the cable cars
3. rafting
4. going hiking
5. eating firefly squid
6. buying tulip bulbs

## My Opinion

I agree ... ○ • I think that Toyama is really cool!

I disagree ... ✕ • We'll visit other famous places.

TAGAKI 30

## Writing Time

**1** Wym's family のように家族旅行で富山県へ行く計画を立てている人になったつもりで A　　　 と B　　　 を入れかえて全文を書こう。

Catchy
Sentences

Facts

Punch
Lines

**2** 上で書いた文を見ないで書いて、見ないで言おう。

Catchy
Sentences

Facts

Punch
Lines

**3** **My Opinion** を参考に自分の意見を書いて、見ないで言おう。

61

## 29 Personality 〈パーソナリティー〉

# Trains
列車

音声がきけます♪

### Sample Sentences

**Catchy Sentences**: When Zim's family goes on a trip, they like to go by train.

**Facts**: Trains are [A] **convenient**. They sit back and relax. They enjoy [B] watching the scenery from the windows.

**Punch Lines**: Let's go right now.

Zim's family

### Words and Phrases

列車の良い点

[A]
1. convenient
2. punctual
3. cheaper
4. safer
5. comfortable
6. friendly

楽しめること

[B]
1. watching the scenery from the windows
2. eating a boxed lunch
3. playing games together
4. reading magazines
5. talking a lot
6. taking a nap

### My Opinion

I agree ... ○ ● We enjoy watching the scenery from the windows, too.

I disagree ... × ● Trains are too boring.

62

## TAGAKI 30

## Writing Time

**1** Zim's family のように家族旅行に行く時、列車で行きたいと思う人になったつもりで **A** と **B** を入れかえて全文を書こう。

**Catchy Sentences**

**Facts**

**Punch Lines**

**2** 上で書いた文を見ないで書いて、見ないで言おう。

**Catchy Sentences**

**Facts**

**Punch Lines**

**3** **My Opinion** を参考に自分の意見を書いて、見ないで言おう。

63

# 30 Winning
Life 〈生活・人生〉

勝つこと

音声がきけます♪

## Sample Sentences

**Catchy Sentences:** Winning is always special.

**Facts:** Last year, the red team won **the dance contest** [A]. They practiced every day. It was so close. They got **a big trophy** [B].

**Punch Lines:** Oh, yeah!

the red team

## Words and Phrases

勝った競技会

A
1. the dance contest
2. the sports day
3. the marathon
4. the play contest
5. the debating contest
6. the long jump rope competition

もらったもの

B
1. a big trophy
2. a big certificate
3. a gold medal
4. nice prizes
5. travel tickets
6. many photos

## My Opinion

**I agree ...** ○ ●We got a big trophy, too.

**I disagree ...** ✕ ●Losing makes people think.

64

TAGAKI 30

## Writing Time

**1** the red team のように勝つことはいつも大切だという人になったつもりで Ⓐ
と Ⓑ を入れかえて全文を書こう。

**Catchy Sentences**

**Facts**

**Punch Lines**

**2** 上で書いた文を見ないで書いて、見ないで言おう。

**Catchy Sentences**

**Facts**

**Punch Lines**

**3** **My Opinion** を参考に自分の意見を書いて、見ないで言おう。

65

コードを読み取れない方や音声をダウンロードしたい方は、右のQRコードまたは以下のURLより、アクセスしてください。
https://www.mpi-j.co.jp/contents/shop/mpi/contents/digital/tagaki30.html

# TAGAKI® 30

| 発　行　日 | ● | 2018年10月11日　初版第 1 刷　　2023年 1 月20日　第11刷 |
|---|---|---|
|  |  | 2023年 3 月20日　 2 版第 1 刷 |
| 執　　　筆 | ● | 松香洋子 |
| 執 筆 協 力 | ● | 近藤理恵子 |
| 英 文 校 正 | ● | Glenn McDougall |
| 編　　　集 | ● | 株式会社カルチャー・プロ |
| イ ラ ス ト | ● | 池田蔵人　石井里果　小林昌子　サノエミコ　仲西太　武曽宏幸 |
| 本文デザイン | ● | DB Works |
| 本 文 組 版 | ● | 株式会社内外プロセス |
| 録音・編集 | ● | 一般財団法人英語教育協議会（ELEC） |
| ナレーション | ● | Erica Williams　Jon Mudryj　Julia Yermakov |
| 写 真 提 供 | ● | アフロ |
| 協　　　力 | ● | 赤松由梨　粕谷みゆき　貞野浩子　野中美恵　宮下いづみ　山内由紀子 |
| 印　　　刷 | ● | シナノ印刷株式会社 |
| 発　　　行 | ● | 株式会社mpi松香フォニックス |
|  |  | 〒151-0053 |
|  |  | 東京都渋谷区代々木2-16-2 第二甲田ビル 2F |
|  |  | fax:03-5302-1652 |
|  |  | URL:https://www.mpi-j.co.jp |

不許複製　All rights reserved.
©2018 mpi Matsuka Phonics inc.
ISBN 978-4-89643-747-8

＊本書で取り扱っている内容は、2017年までの情報をもとに作成しています。
＊QRコードは（株）デンソーウェーブの登録商標です。